CORPORATE

KINGDOM

"Secret Etiquettes: Dominion Through Kingdom Professionalism"

T. L. Davis

Copyright © 2015 by Tami LaDawn Davis

Revelation 17:14

"....: for he is Lord of lords, and King of kings: and they that are with him are <u>called</u>, and <u>chosen</u>, and <u>faithful</u>."

This Book Is Dedicated To:

My mom, Tami Dickerson

&

My beloved inspiration, Alves

**I love you all, so much.
You are true Kings.**

CONTENTS

INTRODUCTION

Chpt I - Times of Dispensation — *3*

Chpt II - Unlocking the King – Dom — *13*

Chpt III - Exercising Quality and Corporate Conduct — *22*

Chpt IV - The Act of Potentate Strategy — *31*

Chpt V - Sovereign Kingship — *38*

Chpt VI - The Thesis of King – Ship — *43*

Chpt VII - Visual (King) Philosophy — *48*

PROPHETIC RELEASE — *55*

ACKNOWLEDGEMENTS

INTRODUCTION

After the world was formed, God efficaciously released an existence beyond the cycles of nature and the human anatomy. Within the person of man, He placed a power called Dominion. Genesis 1:26, "And God said, Let US make man in OUR image, after OUR LIKENESS: And let them have DOMINION...." From where did this supernatural force come? What power is this that God's words take action, and from action they become creation, and from creation they uphold and maintain authority?

Genesis 1:27, "So God created man in HIS IMAGE, in the image of God created he him; male and female created he them." The effervescence of this analysis blots out the physical pulchritude in which God dressed the soul of man. In other words, the gender in which is given to us is neither the image nor likeness God bestowed to his creation. The phrase, "LET US make man in OUR IMAGE," distinctively defines that this image is rather far more intuitive than we can fathom. It is beyond what meets the eye. Its source is not made of flesh and blood, but originated through the counsels of God – like beings and heavenly officials that obtain a supernatural essence. He was speaking to The Godhead.

Revelations 1:6, "And hath MADE US KINGS and priests unto God and his Father: to him be glory and DOMINION forever and ever. Amen." He gave us power, lordship, and kingship over the earth realm. He made us Kings. We are unquestionably behind the mark of our true identity as a body of believers. We are to possess, retrieve, and takeover the land. This is the decree from the ultimate KING himself. Matthew 16:19, "And I will give unto thee the keys to the Kingdom of heaven: and whatsoever thou shalt bind on earth shall be bound in heaven: and whatsoever thou shalt loose on earth shall be loosed in heaven."

We are called to a level of power so immense that it'd shift the very concept in which we view our existence. In order to tap into true Dominion, we must first understand that we are Kings unto the Ultimate KING Himself. Our core existence and purpose is to establish the KINGS – DOM; establishing His Kingdom through unleashing our Kingdom. We must identify it. Establish our kingdoms, build our dynasties, erect our empires, affect our generations, leave legacies, then expire our time as we desire. It is our core duty as Kings to take back, keep, and maintain every facet given to us in the earth realm. Let's LOOSE our DOMINION. This operation is one realm of corporation. This is KINGS Corporation. Let's release Corporate Kingdom!

Chapter I

"Times of Dispensation"

"Understanding the location of time. In the now."

Chpt. 1

Everything is timing. Life is graced within a meter of time. Based upon the events of every era, something extraordinary takes place. Depending on what those events are, it pushes life, cause, and nature forward. It is a core duty to identify the times. In order to effectively operate in Kingdom, we must be able to orchestrate in God's timetable.

His timing is in the dispensation of eternity. He then steps into the earth realm and places eternity into a capsule of transferable times. As descendants of Issachar and embodied pillars housing the Holy Spirit, the discernment of time should be more punctual now than ever. For, we are moving and evolving such as the universe. How be it, we as establishers pinpoint the turn of "church age," now see the conduciveness of a greater need.

This turn of the "Church Century" began before church as we knew it existed. What God has allowed to take place within the timing of this age is, a "ministry metamorphosis." Our cause is growing into a powered catapult for a greater outcome of taking over and launching into true dominion. It's very important to know **WHERE** we are, **WHEN** we are, and **WHO** we are. On our conscience is a spiritual timer, when we're on the verge of a spiritual rise, that timer sets off. It releases a preparation signal for the spirit man to position himself for the next epidemic between the church and the world.

It will be mentioned that we have moved from "Church Reformation" into "Kingdom Revolution."

1500's – The Protestant Movement

In the 1500s was the <u>protestant movement</u>. This began the protest against the Catholic Church. People no longer believed that they had to pay for forgiveness. The priest was selling forgiveness and the mass of that generation believed otherwise, hence, being revealed to "repentance" verses the doctrines of the catholic faith. Because of the cleverness and concepts of the Catholic Church, they became the riches church.

The biggest talk and way of the 1500s was being a part of the protest. You were in "the now" if you were a part of the protest. You had an understanding of knowing that something great and new was coming if you knew that Catholicism wasn't the only way of life. So, in this, the protestant movement was the source of change in the 1500s; leading into the next frame of reform.

1600s – The Puritan Movement

The 1600s brought forth the puritan movement. The big deal was being pure. Living a life of purity and displaying it through your life style was the current way in the 1600s. This generation having proven a point of being pure was God's will, had also generated a platform of what would come next.

1700s – The Holiness Movement

The holiness movement brought forth a reformation in the since of worship and began the African Methodist establishment. This was where we got the format of "camp meetings" from. Also, we got the mindset and ideas of "church organizations" from the customs of the 1700s.

The biggest talk and in "the now" way of life were the holiness establishments of the church age.

1800s – The Faith Healing Movement

In the 1800s, there came an immense change, not only in the way of life, but also within the church. People like D.L. Moody, Smith Wigglesworth, and Billy Sunday were roaming in the land performing "Miracles."

In one instance, Wigglesworth himself approached by a young mother holding her baby; the baby had an unusual illness. She handed Wigglesworth the baby in hopes that God would give him power to perform a miracle for her sick infant. He takes the child, cocks his foot back and kicks him across the platform. The baby never cried, and he never made a sound. When placed back into his mother's arms, she looked into his face and saw that he was healed.

If you operated or supported this way of faith, you were in correct timing with the move of God in this generation.

1900s – The Pentecostal Experience

The 1900s brought forth a turn in the "Church Century." A revelation was given to the logos of what was now getting ready to happen. Pastors were now preaching on The Holy Ghost and people were being filled with His Spirit. Also, this tore down denominational walls. This was called the Pentecostal experience.

If you were a believer in the move of The Holy Ghost and a part of a church that was preaching this talk, you were in "the now."

1950s – The Charismatic Movement

There was a time where the tunes of the Yamahas, Motifs, drums, and Hammonds were considered the "devil's music." Here 50 years later, something very strategic takes place. God, now, has released a revelation to the body that these instruments weren't the devil's music. In fact, it was a great accomplice to the move of the Holy Ghost.

With this change in such an oppressing time, many would come to embrace this change with a supreme level of hope. In the 1950s, if you accepted this change with the host of the body, you were in correct timing.

1970s – The Faith Movement

This movement was very strategic. People like Oral Roberts and Schambach were leading voices in the realm of "show your faith by your works." Oral Roberts build cities to God and Schambach wrote a series of books releasing great revelations of faith.

The preached word streaming through the atmosphere was, "all you need is faith." If you were preaching or believed in this message and this way of life at the time, you were considered to have faith. For those who physically began to erect their faith through actions, they were considered to have great faith.

Having faith was the "in the now" way of church life in the 1970s.

1980s – The Prophetic Movement

January 1, 1980 was an opening of something that would not only change the way in which "church services" flowed, but also the way in which the body viewed God. Especially, His voice. The 1980s brought forth the Prophetic Movement. Now, people were experiencing the "super natural" and being exposed to the governments of the prophetic anointing.

A woman by the name of Kathryn Kuhlman came on the scene talking about the power of the Holy Spirit. She not only prophesied, but she released the prophetic grace leading a remarkable following, many were geared to the prophetic through her ministry.

Other great operators were on the scene, two men by the name of Billy Graham and Benny Hinn, just like Kuhlman, he drew an immense following into the prophetic governments.

The "in the now" way of the 1980s? Only one answer, the Prophetic.

1990s-Mid 2000s – The Apostolic Movement

The 1990s birthed the Apostolic Movement. Church organizations were magnifying the doctrines, orders and supremacy of leading ranks of leadership roles. Another thing that began to emerge within the apostolic movement was the countless Pastors, Bishops, and Televangelists that were developing "mega ministries."

Many headlining preachers, such as; Bishop T. Dexter Jakes, Creflo Dollar, Fred K. Price, Jensen Franklin, Rod Parsley, Juanita Bynum, Paula White, and many more were emerging in the Apostolic faith. Established annual events like Mega Fest, Woman Thou Art Loose, Man Power, Crusades and more were leading signs of change within the "church."

These people not only changed the way in which the apostolic was viewed, but also revealed that there was more to the faith than just strict rules and laws in which to live by. They released a truth that the apostolic held an unstoppable anointing and power that would prepare the body for what was coming next. The Apostolic Movement released an immense not only within the church, but a great deal of a setup in the supernatural.

One of the biggest "in the now" way or talks in the apostolic was mega churches, growing ministries, <u>order</u>, and much more in the spirit that cannot be contained through a one sided view, for many were affected in many ways through this movement.

Mid 2000s – Present Day – Kingdom Establishment

At this very present time something very intriguing is forming in the minds and hearts of millions who can identify the move. In this present age we are experiencing an outstanding change of time. Pulsating through an opened portal is a revelation of Kingdom.

This transformation is so intense that you'll notice many upcoming ministries are identified in some sort of way, by the word *"kingdom."* This move will be a monumental achievement for not only the body of Christ, but for industries established and those that are forth coming.

In this move of Kingdom, one of the primary acknowledgements is the transferring from church reformation, into kingdom revolution. No more saints attending church, only Professional Kings operating in

Corporate Kingdom Principles, establishing market, industrious and universal change.

This is not only the "in the now" move for the way of life, but it's also an enormous, tactical tool for the 21st Century.

The most significant shift in this dispensation of time is the paradigm not only of the individual Kings, but also of every industry and establishment that <u>will be</u> dominated. We are on the lever of a rise so great, that if every nation would come to one mind, the power would be so intense that it'd shake our very galaxy.

Our time is arriving and our release is at hand. What will we do? How will we release the King in us, the King's domain? When will it be released? It is now time to ignite the psychosis with the genuine oils of revelation, sight, to emerge the Pillars of Kingdom, the Corporations of Kingdoms, and the establishment of Kingdom Empire. It's <u>time</u> to do it! No more Church Reformation, time has dispensed into *KINGDOM REVOLUTION*.

Chapter II

"Unlocking The King-Dom"

"Identifying the Governments"

Chapter II

CIA

There is a CIA in you. That is the Creative Invention Ability; the Adam in you. (Genesis 1:26-27) The significance of this government within your corporation or domain is the empowering ability to invent, create, and reason countless ideas for your business and kingdom. The very seed of this skill is the ability to think, form an opinion, and analyze all possibilities.

We are not only king beings, but also science within a rear form. This is the place of conscience that has been locked away from our realization. Why? Because in this place we are as Adam was in the Garden of Eden, <u>before Eve</u>. He operated as in this government of psycho-theory when he named the many animals he encountered. God did not do it. Adam did.

I say to you, Adam Invent! Rise CIA, Rise! Unlock your government; this government is the nucleus of your kingdom. It generates the power of ideas and witty inventions. It forms productions for revenue, tares down walls of limits and restraints, and it identifies the brand for your corporation. The Government of CIA is in you, your Kingdom. Unlock it, take the boundaries off!

___FBI___

There is an FBI in you. This government in you is the Future Business Intellect operation. This is the ability to go beyond current years and establish your corporate kingdom in the bounds of the future. This is also the ability to have a level of futuristic knowledge that will drive your corporation into that next dimension; your kingdom into another realm of power.

This government operation in you is the <u>vision</u> of your kingdom. (Habakkuk 2:2-3) The operation of this government will always keep you in the correct timetable of God. It is the sustainer of your corporation. According to Hosea 4:6, we perish, because we have no knowledge. This knowledge is not just the knowing of information, but it's the ability to obtain valuably information that you may produce and generate accordingly for the better.

Proverbs 29:18 declares, "Where there is no vision, the people perish:" This government within is immensely important. It's the inner voice from the future; it guides, leads, and maintains your kingdom. The Holy Spirit is that voice and He generates valuable knowledge to your FBI operation. This is your Governmental Prophet, the FBI in you. Unlock it, operate, generate!

PES

PES is your Personal Economical Structure. This is a major government factor in your corporation. Your Kingdom CAN NOT expand without it. In your corporation, finances are a truth and a power. Many would not understand. However, the gist is not about how much you obtain, but how you produce and generate to expand your Kingdom.

True Kings do not hesitate to sow or give in order to grow their Kingdom. Kings have such an order in this government that it operates on its own, it flows with smoothness. Kings with a realm and mind of dominion barely focus on attracting revenue. They focus on placing revenue in places that their Corporation AND Kingdom will **TAKE OVER**.

This principle is found in II Corinthians 9:6-12. II Corinthians 9:12 declare, *"For the administration of this service not only supplieth the want of the saints, but is abundant also by many thanksgivings unto God."* This government within your corporation magnifies the epitome of why it exists in the first place. Your Kingdom is only in place to establish the ultimate Kingdom. That is the Kingdom of God.

Your operation of PES is the hand that grabs and makes provision for your corporation. This government is formed to birth out your dominion. Yes, riches are involved, yes, fame is involved, yes, your brand is on the line. BUT, the key purpose, the main reason is to bring into fold, the Kingdom of God in the earth realm. Unlock this government, your corporation needs it. If you cannot adopt the very <u>primary principle</u> of this government, you will choke; even kill the potential power of your Kingdom.

Matthew 13:31-33 and Luke 13:18-21 shows this primary principle through a parable that Jesus releases. Summarized, He declares, that *the Kingdom of Heaven is like a <u>SEED</u>, which <u>a man</u> took, and <u>SOWED</u> in his field. But when it <u>GROWS</u> it is the greatest and becomes a tree where the birds build their nests among the branches and dwell there. The Kingdom of Heaven is also, like a <u>GRAIN</u>, which <u>a woman</u> took, and placed in three measures of flour, until they <u>BAKED/EXPANDED</u> into the intended bread:*

In Kingdom Ordinance, the only way to expand your corporation is to sow! There is no other way. <u>It's Principle!</u> Jesus Himself released this. The <u>operation of expansion</u> is in this government. The King in you is recognized by this operation. This is the only parable where Jesus specified the gender of each Kingdom. He specified strongly, to clarify the principle across the board. It works no other way.

Unlock it, it's in you. You King, this government in you can only operate on this primary principle, first: You have it in you, release it!

POA

POA is the Presentation of Appearance. It's the face and quality of your Kingdom Corporation. This government operates in a very unique manner. It produces the essence of your kingdom. It is the pulsating release. The <u>operation of display</u> is in this government. Every encounter, rise and fall resides in this operation.

In order for your Kingdom to generate <u>high quality value</u>, you must master the etiquette of conduct and character to produce attraction for the establishment. Your Kingdom should release nothing less than **<u>FRESH EXCELLENCE</u>**. Hence, your establishment is a replica of that of the ultimate. Colossians 1:16-17 shows the resemblance of how and why your Kingdom is made in replication to that of the Kingdom of God. However, this government not only establishes the identity of your corporation, but it also classifies the niche or niches it possesses.

According to I Corinthians 14:40 and vs. 33, the primary principle of this government is that of an <u>Organizational Paradigm</u>. It is imperative that order is a major aspect within this government in order to profoundly present your corporation in the stance of studiousness it obtains. This will not only allow your Kingdom to standout, but it will shine light on the peculiar quality this government generates. It is the face that the outer Worlds, Cultures, and Kingdoms will embrace or reject.

This government is the liaison of your Kingdom. When in congress with other Kings, this government is the first to project, represent your corporation. Release it, unlock it, and maximize it. This governmental operation is the underling balance of the successes of your Kingdom. It's in YOU!

CORPORATE KINGDOM STRUCTURE

(Model I)

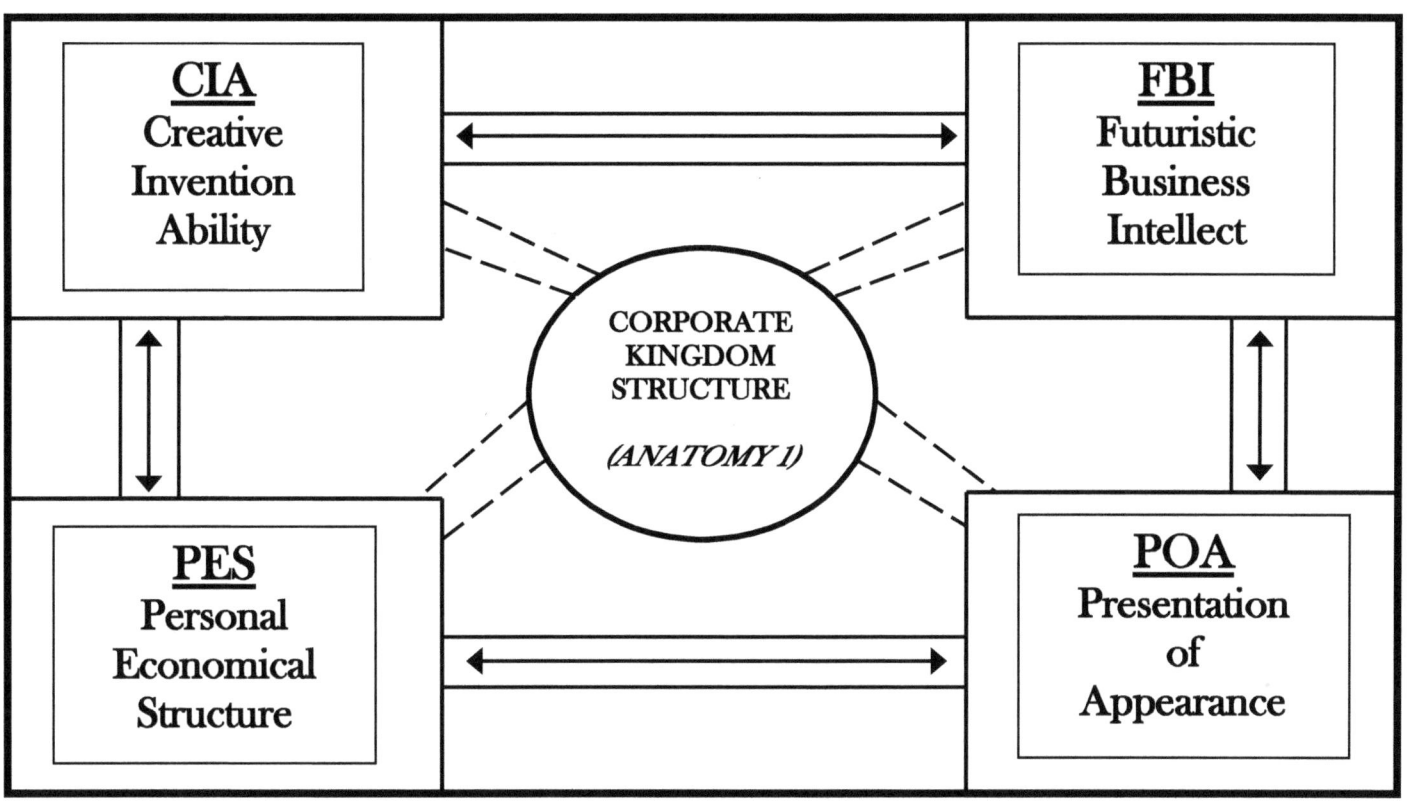

21

CHAPTER III

"EXERCISING *QUALITY* AND CORPORATE *CONDUCT*"

"The Application of QUALITY through your Corporation"

Chapter III

There is not only an immense need for Corporate Kings to reside in high places, but for Corporate Kings to display a level of "debonair power" in the midst of industries that'll place the very core of these establishments in the palm of their hands. In this, the act or corporate operation of "TAKING OVER" is in effect across the board.

Yet, magnifying the projection of Luke 2:46-50. The very first stems erected from Jesus' idiosyncrasies are that of *unusual knowledge* and *peculiar wit*. This display of "Kingdom Debonair" was not only unique for a twelve year old boy speaking with doctors, but for the wisdom being dispersed; He subliminally showed His true power. A power so rare, but yet so igniting that the *atmospheres* came subject to the dominating force and the causality approach from each witness was in awe. Luke 2:47 declared, *"And all that heard him were astonished at his understanding and answers."* In other words, Jesus presented His Kingdom in a form of QUALITY and on a level so riveting that He retrieved the atmospheres with no imp of restraint. This was a notable view of the corporate operation of *taking over*. So explosive, that the minds of these doctors were in the "palm of His hand."

That is the primary place, the source, the mind. It's the MIND. Highlighted in Proverbs 21:22, *"A wise man scaleth the city of the mighty, and casteth down the strength of the confidence thereof."* Yet argumentative, the strength of any man is the mind. Hence, scientifically, the physical body cannot function without the mind/ brain no matter the state of the function. Agreeable. A form of a prerequisite of *the city*, according to Proverbs 21:22 is the structure of the life of the one in the high place of the corporation in the corporate world.

However, in Corporate Kingdom, the first tool of method to taking over is the display of *King-Dom Debonair*. One must become a tactician in this operation. The core of each territory to aim for is the mind. [The King and his Kingdom are *the city*. The operation of the mind is *the strength*. The source of the force of what causes the mind to operate the way it does is *the confidence*.] That is the BELIEF SYSTEM. When you diagnose the operation of the belief system, you have the vital view of what keeps the counter-kingdom afloat.

How do Kings Takeover Kings-Dom? How do we "scale?" Unfolding the method to unlocking the secret skill, you follow the sacred pattern of Jesus. Luke 2:46, *"And it came to pass, that after three days they found him in the temple, sitting in the midst of doctors, both HEARING THEM and ASKING THEM questions."*

1.) He learned their <u>mental expansion.</u>

2.) He rhetorically planted/ made <u>His mark.</u>

3.) He released, with a WIT, mysterious nuggets of wisdom from an unknown source.

4.) He gave them a glimpse of a rare form of power <u>beyond their mental capacity</u>. Kingdom. (His Kingdom.)

5.) He displayed and released by way of suave verbiage. In other words, <u>King speech</u>. He spoke like a King. His confidence.

He learned the customs of their operations and executed accordingly

As Kings, if we are going to establish Corporate Kingdom in the corporate world, we must establish the science of their entities. Let's do it, but first it must be approached in the art of quality. This is the first step in transitioning as a corporate body, all across the globe from "Church Reformation into Kingdom Establishment." Let's establish the science of perfecting quality.

The Facts of Quality
(Taking a look through the eyes of the corporate world/ their way)

> *QUALITY– Basic individual nature, a basic characteristic, <u>grade of excellence</u>, <u>high social rank</u>, <u>something that sets a person or thing apart</u>:*

Corporate World Synonyms:
1. *VALUE*
2. *PRIDE*
3. *RESPECT*
4. *REVERANCE*

KINGDOM APPLICATION

As a **Christian** Business Leader (King), you have one thing within that sets you above and beyond your counterparts. If unlocked, recognized, pursued, and maintained; the outcome of your success will always excel at a more, vast rate. That one thing is the gift of sight. You have the ability to advance any organization, corporation, and team. Because you see beyond, you navigate the course to success. It's the secret in generating QUALITY.

In the corporate world there is a level of class and etiquette that resides in two forums. Power and position. In other words, since the beginning, leadership has always been identified by a level of conduct and visible principle. That is the outward expression of how they viewed the importance and QUALITY of their role as a leader.

Intellect and Presentation

The power of your wit will control the flow of your ambition. It is in your conscience that you must establish the value of your role as a leader in the 21st Century Corporate World. Whether it is of your own or of another establishment, only you can erect the value of your professional essence.

"Basic Arts For Perfecting Quality"

INTELLECT
Intellect is the power of knowing.

PRESENTATION
Presentation is something set forth for attention.

In order for every aspect of your life to be filled with the richness and character of class portrayed in the business world; you must develop **quality thinking**.

If you combine intellect, presentation and quality; the outcome will birth a psychosis reform of etiquette. Mastering quality is the first step towards proper etiquette. It shows that everything you do, you do it with a belief in excellence.

As a **Kingdom Establisher**, what makes you standout is the *presentation* of your work ethic, the *intellect* of your professional forum, and the *quality* in which you display your ambition.

27

APPLICATION OF QUALITY

(Methods & exercises for enhancement of professional etiquette)

VERBAIGE:

(Corporate Talk)

* What Business are you in?

- I am in partnership with ___, by way of ___.

* Interesting, How's that going for you?

- As of now we're pushing forth ___, and it'll attract ___.

It is important to always keep up with the progress of the company you're in partnership with.

When faced with inquiry about your corporation, never talk about the negatives. Highlight the latest project and the progress its making/ made.

QUALITY THROUGH PHYSICALITY

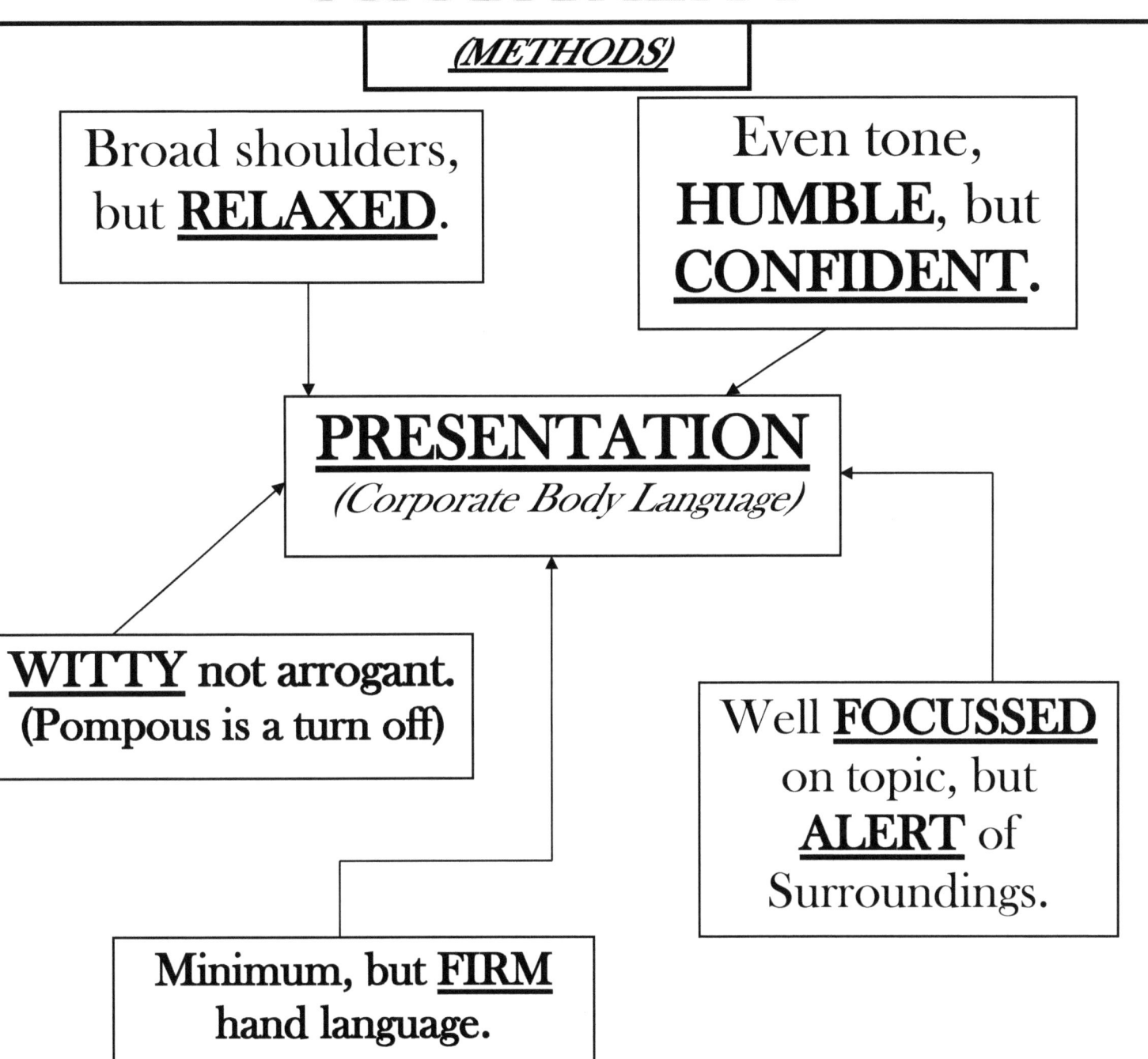

(METHODS)

Broad shoulders, but **RELAXED**.

Even tone, **HUMBLE**, but **CONFIDENT**.

PRESENTATION
(Corporate Body Language)

WITTY not arrogant. (Pompous is a turn off)

Well **FOCUSSED** on topic, but **ALERT** of Surroundings.

Minimum, but **FIRM** hand language.

<u>Don't show your ambition, BE your ambition.</u>

Corporate Kings in the midst of counter – corporations must synch with the best or highest level of etiquette. This is an advantage, and secret skill in having true dominance in the effect of establishing the ultimate Kingdom in the corporate world and the mind of their kings. We must do it.

CHAPTER IV

"The Act of *Potentate* Strategy"

The Tools of Tactic Etiquette

Chapter IV

As Corporate Kings endeavoring in corporate – world *operations*, we must manifest the ultimate Kings-Dom with strategic execution. We have this power with unlimited access to a source with unlimited power. We are Kings on earth, releasing our Kingdom for the ultimate KING and HIS KINGDOM. We have the ingenuity of a very rare form that will expand our Corporate Kingdom Operations into territories of governmental, scientific, educational, industrious, worldwide, entertainment, political, economical, psychological, and hundreds of more establishments. This cannot be done without <u>potent</u>, <u>strategic</u>, calibrated methods of etiquette.

I Timothy 6:15, *"Which in his times he shall shew, who is the blessed and <u>POTENTATE</u>, the KING of Kings, and LORD of Lords."* The ultimate Potentate is the KING of us Kings and LORD of us Lords. We're made after His image and His likeness to manifest His dominion in the earth realm. This is why anyone preaching "God doesn't need you" should reconsider that analysis. Yet, confrontational. However, the verbiage should change to "God has need of you, but if you are not willing, He will choose another."

With that being said, you must make clarification of your Kingdom; seeing that it replicates the ultimate Kingdom and not the kingdom of darkness. In that factor, when entering counter – kingdoms, you must make strategic entrances and approaches. Synch carefully, this is the first <u>operation of establishment</u>, making your mark. It is important to <u>visibly</u> display tactical etiquette when in the midst of counter – kings.

There are methods of approach and strategies of tactics to operate in a realm of etiquette that will ignite the very essence of Corporate Kingdom Operations. *It is another secret skill in taking over.* Let's take a look at some methodic skills we must exercise in corporate world operations.

Mounting a Platform
(Methods of Approach)

GREETING FORUM

Greet entire platform. It shows respect for the roster, event, and panel. You produce a crisp generosity towards your reputation and you leave an intriguing impression.

OVAL APPROACH

Whether it is your right or left shoulder the proper etiquette form of greeting the roster is the sideways approach. The audience should see your profile. It gives respect, respect to your atmosphere and it sets the tone for your person.

SITTING

DON'T BE HASTY! Ask politely if <u>empty</u> seat is occupied. When sitting, politely say, "Excuse me." Watch, examine your platform. Feel the tone already set.

(Because you are a King-Dom operator, if the atmosphere isn't conducive; take charge in the spirit. <u>Command</u>, <u>Declare</u>, and <u>Decree</u>.)

<u>*It could save, make, or break business*</u>

Giving & Receiving Business Cards
(The first form of identity)

RECEIVING	GIVING
When receiving a business card, take a look and ask, "And these are the means of communication?"	Your business card is the <u>**DOORWAY**</u> into <u>**YOUR CORPORATION**</u>.
<u>Do not</u> put it away quickly. Hold it. When conversation is completed and it's time to shake hands; neatly place it into your blazer breast pocket, wallet, or portfolio.	Be prepared, alert, and ready! Know who to give your card to.
	Give it face up. Give it with debonair.

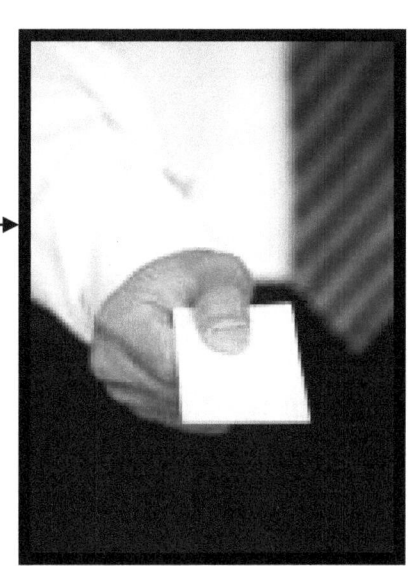

HAND SHAKE
(Methods & Theories of Approach)

VS.

A forceful and even over excited approach shows competition. It gives a subliminal message as an attempt to make one inferior, to want control.

(The <u>HEAD to HEAD approach</u>)

<u>A big don't do</u>

DEFEAT

Lack of eye contact and uneven head level shows intimidation. You show low to none ambition and a lack of confidence.

<u>Don't do</u>

PROFESSIONAL

A square look in the eyes. Warm smile, don't cheese - it shows mental vulnerability/ easily persuaded. NO dip (hand). NEVER use left hand - shows low class, ONE <u>slight</u> shake. Nod head—shows approval of presentation.

HEEL COCKED
Means risk taker within means of reality.
A go getter.

36

These skills are very important to exercise. It is beyond the physical eye what's really going on. Our unique system, Kingdom Establishment, is designed to prolifically execute the operation in which we are mandated to transpire the powers of Corporate Kingdom Industry. We have no other choice but to move in excellence with tact.

The ultimate KING will operate in no other way, but by excellence according to I Corinthians 14:40. This is "principle" indeed. I Corinthians 14:40, "*Let all things be done <u>decently</u> and <u>in order</u>.*" He operates by this standard and as Kings we MUST operate by this standard, dogmatically. It's Corporate Kingdom Principle!

CHAPTER V

(THE MOMENT OF POWER)

"SOVEREIGN KINGSHIP"

"Possessing You - King"

Chapter V

We have viewed ourselves through the wrong perception for centuries. We've viewed ourselves as men for far too long. In the state of man, we think as men. In the state of Kings, we visualize as Kings. We are forces incredibly charged with authority. It is the Ultimate King's desire for His creation to come into realization with whom and what we really are. Ephesians 3:9, *"And to make all men SEE what is the FELLOWSHIP of the MYSTERY, which from the beginning of the world hath been hid in GOD, who created ALL things by Jesus Christ:"* It is His decree that we come into true light of our supernatural identity and BECOME IT.

We have a Kingship not only in the earth realm, but also in heaven. The powers of reigning over territories are ours and not intended for the forces of darkness. He designed it for us to make known His KINGDOM in every realm and every world. Ephesians 3:10, *"To the intent that now unto the principalities and powers in heavenly places might be KNOWN......"* The King wants His kings to reside in the powers that He's ordained. You are a King and Lord over territories in which you may have not come into contact quite yet. The territories and principalities we are to possess are in many forms; they are in systems, industries, movements, organizations, governments, branches, geographical locations, lands, seas, realms, channels, portals, anointing and many other facets.

Arise! Establish your LEGAL right and unveil yourself. Come out of hiding and be released! KING! I quicken you in mortality and in spirit. This is YOUR MOMENT! You have been blessed, pledged and commemorated for your reign to come into fruition. The dynasty waits. The empire yearns to break forth! By the authority placed within your lips, DECREE IT! True Kings master the art of Decree! DO IT and make it well! YOU have JURISDICTION and PROCLOMATION over every principality you own and over every realm you possess!

This is the mind of God concerning you. Philippians 2:5, *"Let THIS MIND be in you, which was also in Christ Jesus:"* This thinking, this way of life, this measure of faith, may it be revealed in you completely! Philippians 1:6, *"Being CONFIDENT of this very thing, that he which hath BEGUN a GOOD work in you will PERFORM it until the day of Jesus Christ:"* Hebrews 12:2, *" Looking unto Jesus the AUTHOR and FINISHER of our FAITH....."*

At this time right where you are, He's revealing it. He's making it clear to you, your true identity and rank in the earth and worlds. I put apostolic and prophetic pressures on YOU, NOW in the power of the HOLY SPIRIT! I command your Angelic Assistances to make your atmosphere conducive, your current realm conducive, your current anointing conducive! May the ministry of your corporation be immense in abundance, and abundantly blessed! The seal of the Lord of host SHALL perform this!

I release the glory, that the entrance of your royalty is sealed and established! The KING of GLORY and the LORD strong and MIGHTY stand in agreement! BREAK OUT KING! Complete the metamorphosis, transform, grow, CHANGE from man into King! Establish your Superior Power! I arrest every demonic entity that would barricade your psychosis from excelling into your Kingship! I unlock the oracles of heaven concerning your legislation, may they be upon your head! May it be one of your crowns!

This is and it is INDEED! I bar every satanic encroachment and high jacking of your identity as King and Lord over your region! I flow into prophetic veins and I pronounce your Corporation and Kingdom! May your angels operate in justice, as you excel, may they excel! I command that every divine inspiration from the Word of God flows freely through the operations of your Kingdom! May your King-Dom be established! May every Co-King in our Corporate Kingdom venerate you and may you return veneration! I command every goal to be one, every mission to be completed, and every economical status to be filled with the riches of our Ultimate KING!

May He prosper your governments, bless your operations, empower your structures, anoint your tactics, promote your strategies, strengthen your angels, protect your portals, expand your dominion, further your decrees, enlarge the mind of your corporation, seal your territories with His declaration, place a throne on all of your principalities, make His mark in your reign, and release His all consuming fires to destroy every counter – king or kingdom that would rise against you!

I finalize this verdict! I prophetically release this decree in proper timing and course! And it is so, even as heaven stands in agreement, we LOOSE you, King, in Jesus name!

CHAPTER VI

"The Thesis of King-*Ship*"

"The Establishment of Corporate Empire"

Chapter VI

"EMPIRE"

Because we are Kings under the rule of an Ultimate KING and His Kingdom, it is of great need that we generate the reign of our Lordship and the powers that we possess in a manner that'll expose our CORPORATE dominance. He is the head of our Kingdoms, operations, governments, and territories of reign. Colossians 2:10, *"………which is the HEAD of ALL principalities and power:"* This shows the essence of our Kingdom Empire and Powers of Legislation.

The reign of this heavenly administration is so compacted with power, once mastered; it will immobilize the operations of every counter existence. We have advantage because of the HEAD organization in which we belong. No more oppressed and mundane progression, only prosperous, effective transactions for our sole purpose. Because the KING of us Kings bare many titles, our branches of operation and legalities are far more efficient if we fashion our individual dynasties after His structures.

The pulse of our Kingdoms MUST pattern the heartbeat of the Ultimate Kingdom's tempo. It must synch and replicate accordingly. Our ALLEGIANCE to our Corporate Kingdom Empire must show immensely! This is the outward operation of KEA (*Kingdom Empire ALLEGIANCE.)*

"SHIPS"

The *unit* in which the specification of your royal identity rest, is very peculiar:

There are many different units within the SHIPS of our Corporation. These ships are the states or conditions of our Corporate Empire. Within the structure of each ship there is a special unitary with a specific operation:

"Prophetic Unitary"

There are Kings who fall into this unit. Kings of Supernatural and Prophetic governments have a very unique, gravitational pull on atmospheres. These Kings flow in accurate and precise *timing*.

"Governing Unitary"

The entities of this unit are very strategic. Kings with the special ability to maintain a high level of order would be in this unit. Some of the strongest of their qualities are revealed in the manner in which they flow in their operations, systems, governments and structures.

"Apostolic Unitary"

Kings designed for this unit are very rare. Their abilities are well rounded, but the concise measure of their core existence is in the volume of a *Reformer*. These particular Kings shift theological and theoretic truths into newer levels of realization. These Kings ignite the universe with impeccable change.

"Militancy Unitary"

Kings that fall into this unit are natural warriors. They build special infantries purposed for warfare within their Kingdoms. They specialize in destroying and taking over counter – kingdoms of darkness. The infantries they establish in their corporations build walls of protection. On these walls, they watch and discern counter – forces.

There are many units within our Corporate Kingdom Empire. The empire in which is set forth from the Ultimate KING is to make a distinct difference between the establishment of our Highness and the counter – establishment of darkness. With our way of Corporate Kingdom FAITH, we are to multiply our empire by displaying our light in the realm darkness.

>Revelations 21:24, *"And the nations of them which are saved shall walk in the light of it: and the <u>KINGS of the EARTH</u> do bring their glory and honor into it."*

CHAPTER VII

"Visual

(King)

Philosophy"

"Kingdom Perspective"

GRID:

The Grid of Take Over:

This grid is a visualization of what it looks like in the arts of *"taking over."* This grid is designed that we may carry out all we o as Kings over the earth with circumspection.

The Art of Making Your Mark

The Grid of Take Over

Model I

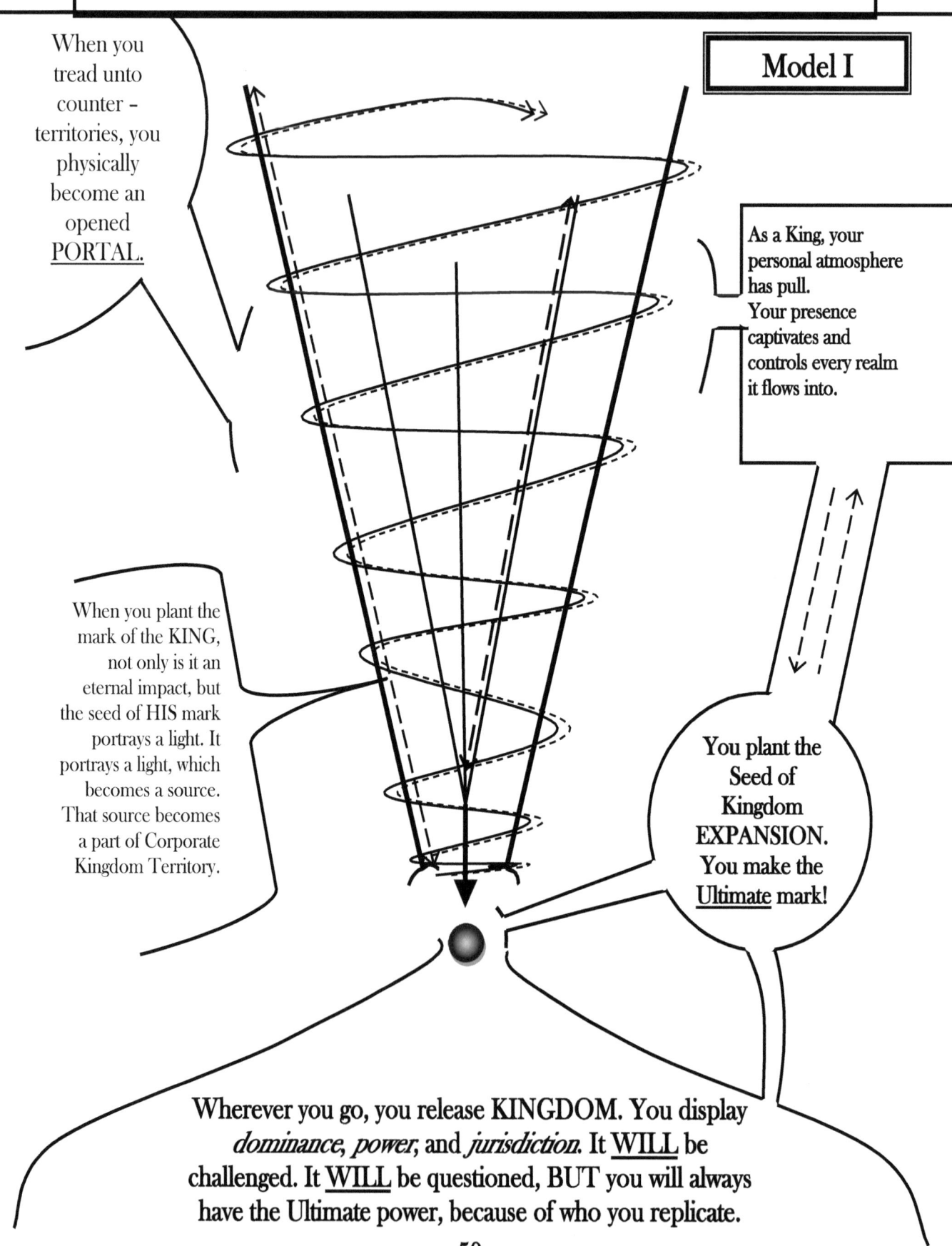

When you tread unto counter-territories, you physically become an opened PORTAL.

As a King, your personal atmosphere has pull. Your presence captivates and controls every realm it flows into.

When you plant the mark of the KING, not only is it an eternal impact, but the seed of HIS mark portrays a light. It portrays a light, which becomes a source. That source becomes a part of Corporate Kingdom Territory.

You plant the Seed of Kingdom EXPANSION. You make the Ultimate mark!

Wherever you go, you release KINGDOM. You display *dominance, power,* and *jurisdiction*. It WILL be challenged. It WILL be questioned, BUT you will always have the Ultimate power, because of who you replicate.

CHART:

The Geo – King Chart of Power:

I Corinthians 4:20, *"For the Kingdom of God is not in word, but in Power."* This synopsis vision is an insight of the overview of the Kingdoms in the earth realm and the operations of powers.

Geographical Realm Dominance

- It is extremely important to pinpoint every aspect of your province.

- When in crisis you must unlock the portal/ portals of access to *Geographical Domain Calibration*.

- The collective thesis of your locations is precisely the undertone of what operation or operations that maintain the systems of these boundaries.

- You MUST keep open the FBI (Future Business Intellect) governmental channels to stay in tune with the moves of the Ultimate organization.

- You should always want every area of your Kingdom to be in synch with that of the Ultimate. HIS way is righteous and filled with HIS MAJESTY.

WEB:

Geographical Realm Domain:

This particular visualization is a display of main points to keep in the frontal lobe of your psyche. As a King, it is of necessity to know the tools and sacred duties of maintain your Kingdom with high levels of *Quality*.

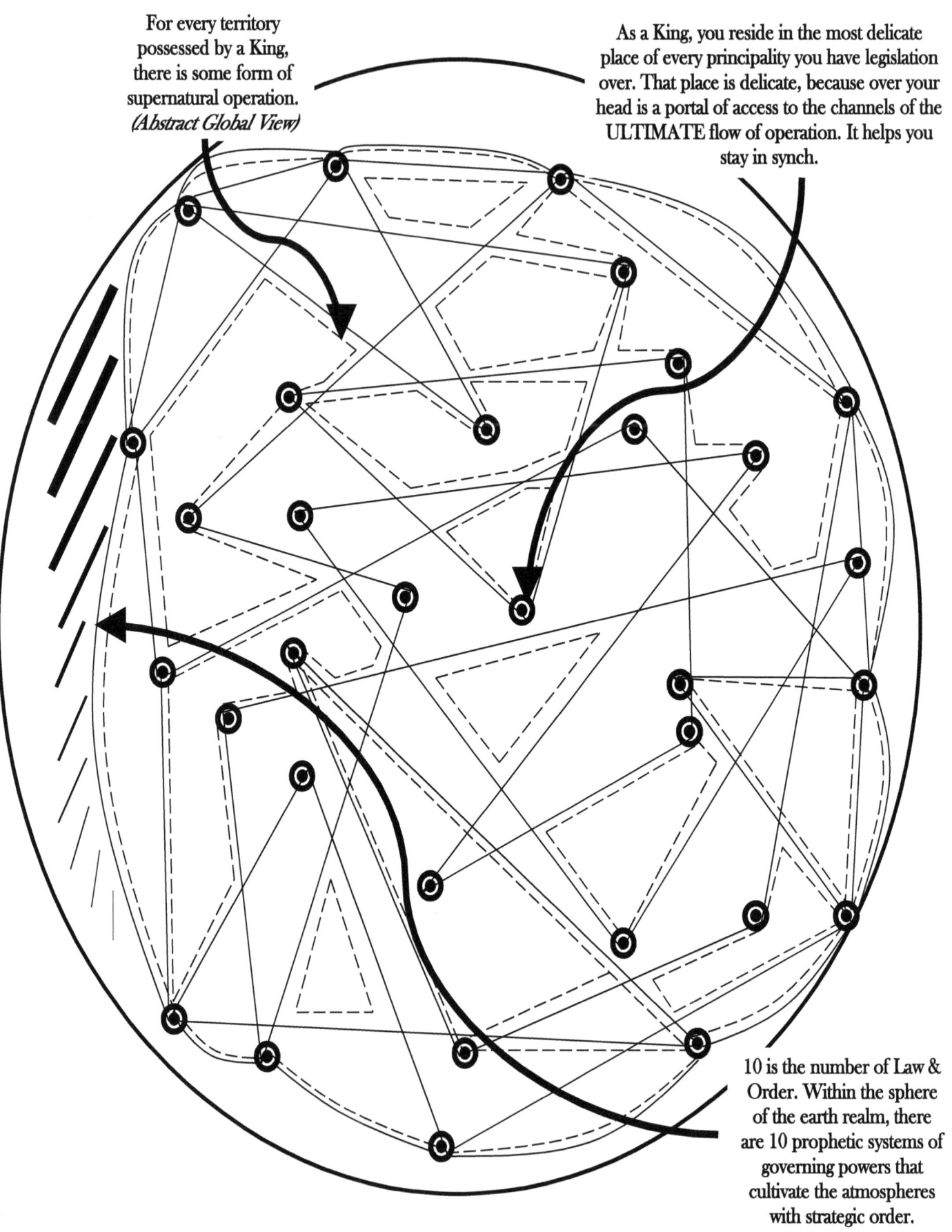

For every territory possessed by a King, there is some form of supernatural operation. *(Abstract Global View)*

As a King, you reside in the most delicate place of every principality you have legislation over. That place is delicate, because over your head is a portal of access to the channels of the ULTIMATE flow of operation. It helps you stay in synch.

10 is the number of Law & Order. Within the sphere of the earth realm, there are 10 prophetic systems of governing powers that cultivate the atmospheres with strategic order.

"The Geo-King Chart of Power"

PROPHETIC RELEASE

1:27 AM   October 29, 2014

The world is going to come at the mercy of God. The body of Christ will have dominion over Economics, Education, Sports, and Politics, the work force, trades with other countries, Military Personnel, and Capitol Hill.

The Church will be the matriarch and cornerstone of the world. China will be a major submission, along with many, hundreds of other countries. They will follow the infinite wisdom from God, given to the saints that will mold and shape the government and economic flow of this world.

All nations, colors, and creeds will come to know that our sole existence is to establish the Kingdom of God in every system founded in this world. They will know that what Jesus established is not a religion, movement, nor occult, but a way of life; a culture.

They will reach out for help and counsel concerning their economics, businesses, educations, political structures, presidential and congress establishments, sports, music and media, and science and technology developments. It will be common for CEOs to call on prophets with business intellect to consult on major deals and acquisitions, for capitol hill to call on ministers with teachings on how to reconstruct economic flows and statuses, for apostles to be called on to pray before presidents and congress conducts their meetings. It'll even be common for evangelist and revivalist to be called on to anoint and pray for new presidents and their families at their inaugurations.

It'll be common for presidents to have a meeting with many pastors about their deacons being ambassadors for their countries to travel and make peace.
There will be a time when the world will have revival and leaders in high places will take on holiness and righteousness.

*Honesty will flow from the governments and powers of this world. Truth and freedom will reign in court systems. Blood thirsty councilmen will come to naught. Our national anthems in all the world will be lead of a prayer and followed of a prayer. Justice will reign and judgment will be righteous, says the Lord. And it is so and so shall it be. Amen:

ACKNOWLEDGEMENTS

I'd like to take this time to thank The KING of my life, God my Father, my Lord and Savior Jesus Christ, my best Friend, Teacher, Help and Guide the Holy Spirit. You guys are incredibly awesome! I'm in awe of your voice, touch, and presence. Thank you for entrusting me to be a steward over your mysteries.

I'd like to thank my mother, Tami D. Dickerson. Thank you for being understanding and patient. I love you very much. To Alves, you are the best and dearest person in my life. I love you to the moon and back, you were the first person to ever truly understand me. I'm still amazed by it. To my dear friend and Pastor, Pastor Jason Coakley, thank you for your blessing. You are an igniting individual. To Josh, I love you baby bro, this is to inspire you to tap into all that God has for you. DO IT! To Andre' and Sophia, thank you and I love you guys! Thank you, to my father, Andrew Davis, I love you.

To Bishop K.D. Nesmith, thank you for being the very first fountain of wisdom in my life. To Eric Nesmith, my father, I love you and thank you for your hand in raising me in the church. To Ingrid Graham, Thank you for being my genius teacher. You've deeply impacted my life. To Mrs. Katrina Cohen, Thank you so much for being an inspiration.

    Accolades to: Devorah Nataline Davis, I love you my niece, Robyn Wilson, I love you Auntie, Briahna Dickerson, Kionne Epps, Courtney "Doestacks" Dickerson, I LOVE you guys so much. God has tons in store for you all! Kerri Bradford, Ernie Bradford, I love you all. Zaria, Zion, and Zaylen, I love you guys. To the Horton Family, Burroughs Family, Dickerson Family, Davis Family, Williams Family, and Deas Family; I love you all. I pray for true unity. Greatness is upon you guys. To Sheila Rogers, you Prophet! You will always be my sister and friend! Finally, to every individual, nation, color and creed, this is to ignite the flames of Kingdom - bound ingenuity in you! There's a KING in YOU!

I Timothy 2:2

"For <u>kings</u>, and for ALL that are in <u>authority</u>; that we may lead a quiet and peaceable life in all godliness and honesty."